ULTIMA THULE

DAVIS McCOMBS

WITH A FOREWORD BY W. S. MERWIN

YALE UNIVERSITY PRESS / NEW HAVEN & LONDON

Published with assistance from a grant to honor James Merrill.

Designed by Mary Valencia
Set in Cochin and Futura type by
The Composing Room of Michigan, Inc.
Printed in the United States of America by Thomson-Shore,
Dexter, Michigan.

Library of Congress Cataloging-in-Publication Data

McCombs, Davis, 1969–
Ultima thule / Davis McCombs; with a foreword by W. S.
Merwin.
    p.   cm. — (Yale series of younger poets; v. 94)
ISBN 0-300-08316-5 (alk. paper) — ISBN 0-300-08317-3
(paper: alk. paper)
1. Mammoth Cave (Ky.) — Poetry.   2. Caves — Kentucky —
Poetry.   I. Title.   II. Series.
PS3563.C34348 U48 2000
811'.54 — dc21
99-052548

A catalogue record for this book is available from the British
Library.

The paper in this book meets the guidelines for permanence
and durability of the Committee on Production Guidelines for
Book Longevity of the Council on Library Resources.

10 9 8 7 6 5 4 3 2 1

FOR
MY PARENTS
GEORGE AND JANICE McCOMBS
AND
FOR
CAROLYN

CONTENTS

II. THE RIVER AND UNDER THE RIVER

III. THE DARK COUNTY

FOREWORD

In the past few years a number of gifted young poets have presented collections of poems related to some single theme or subject or image. This is not without precedent: it is easy to think of forerunners, from the Greek pastoral poets, to Petrarch, to the Spoon River Anthology. Why there should be this recurrence now is something we can only guess at. It may have to do with an urge for a different scope from that of short poems standing by themselves; for the broad canvas of narrative, without linear continuity.

One thing that happens when poems cluster in this way around some common formation or feeling or circumstance is that the recurring subject, poem by poem, becomes a primal metaphor which in turn informs each of the separate poems to some degree, and the poems come to pick up reflections of each other.

The ruling image of Davis McCombs's *Ultima Thule* is the cave. Before turning to Freud or Plato, and their lights on the subject, it is well to know that McCombs has a very specific cave, or caves, in mind — their topography, their history, and the history of human acquaintance with them. He lives in Kentucky and when he presented this manuscript he was working as a park ranger at Mammoth Cave National Park. The known and the unknown of that vast complex of riddled limestone, as it exists in the earth and in the minds of those who have come to it, awake and asleep and in all the tenses of language, are the setting for his poems. The more apparently defined and practical and rational the viewer's approach to this setting, the more evident it is that what informs the references, all of them, is the underworld. We know immediately that the main ground is unknowable, that what we seem to know of it is immeasurably small, fragile, and flickering. Only a little of it can even be spoken of directly. But since this unknowable bourne underlies all the surface accounts and illumination that pass over it, they themselves refer to it, even in telling of themselves.

The human figure, or the human shadow, that goes ahead with a light through the passages of *Ultima Thule* is that of Stephen Bishop, born in 1820, a slave of Dr. John Croghan, who owned Mammoth Cave from 1839 to 1849. (The idea of "owning" this sunless labyrinth seems even stranger after reading McCombs's book than before.) In a prefatory note McCombs describes Bishop's two decades of work as a guide in the cave, during which he helped explore countless new passageways and became something of a tourist attraction himself.

So McCombs, employed as a ranger at the cave, is retracing a predecessor in Stephen Bishop — a figure of the known and of the unknown. And in the first sequence of poems in the collection Bishop speaks. He does so, inevitably, in a later voice, from a later shadow.

McCombs's own language is quiet, understated, delicate as a hand exploring a tunnel in the dark, and it remains so whether he is writing in the voice of Bishop or in his own, with his unfinished questions, some of which may have been Bishop's before him. McCombs's search for Bishop, his conjuring up of Bishop, and Bishop's questions, as he imagines them, come back to him like an echo of his voice in the caverns. "Am I the letters or the hand that made them?" his figure of Stephen Bishop asks, in the book's first poem, speaking of the names forming from the soot of a candle on the cave walls, as he is learning to write. Bishop's vocabulary, in the poems, has become that of an articulate, highly literate successor, part remnant and part persona, who in speaking of the waxing of the moon can allude to "everything cognate to her nature." Yet the vocabulary, in his voice, is not forced nor obtrusive, and what presents it, the author and the elusive forerunner share. The later figure — the author — explores the questions from a dif-

ferent perspective in the "outside" world, in the book's penulti-
mate poem, "Stephen Bishop's Grave," where he recognizes
Bishop's elusiveness, the other side of his shadow, as something
integral to the search itself, and ends listening without expecta-
tion, aware that a search for summary must come to accept that
there is no such thing. The poem itself, even in the quiet of its tone,
is as close to a summary as the book comes.

Stephen Bishop's Grave

It took four summers here for me to realize
the cave looped back under the Old Guide
Cemetery, that what was mortal floated
in a crust of brittle sandstone or leaked
into the darkest rivers and was caving still.
I went that drizzling night to stand
where the paper-trail he left had vanished:
woodsmoke, mist, a mossed-over name.
I knew enough by then to know that he,
of all people, would prefer the company of rain
to my own, but I went anyway, thinking
of my pale inventions, and stood a long time,
vigilant for his shadow in my own,
his voice as it differed from the wind.

In the poems in Bishop's voice, McCombs gives us a language that
is, necessarily, his own, and in doing it plainly and without empha-
sis he creates a haunting, echoing distance, a sound from some
unidentifiable place. He presents a simplicity of words not of mind.

There is a further echo in the poems that are set in the voice or
in the footsteps of Bishop. They are the length, and they suggest

the meter, of sonnets: a sonnet sequence, or an allusion to one, and the classical theme of the sonnet sequence is love, the unfinishable relation. The poems of the book's second section, flaring up into moments of the history of the cave, are in a more rapid line, the pace of notation:

Near Mummy Valley a flat slab
propped upright and markings —
turtle? dancing figure? map of the cave?
Twenty centuries and only one moment
when burnt torch end scraped limestone . . .

And the moment is in the poem:

. . . trace of what held heat, what is mine.

The history defers to one of the great admonitory shadows, Floyd (Floyd Collins), cave explorer, trapped in a nearby cave in 1925, dying in the dark, immensely famous for a while, then another monosyllabic echo, in the poems of Donald Finkel, in our time, and now in those of McCombs, who glimpses him at two moments: when Floyd enters the cave in the winter, February 1925, and then the moment that is all that was afterward — the laying out, the exploitation, the leaching away.

The book's third section moves through time in the upper world of Kentucky farmland and forest, and the recurring awareness of the caverns, the night, and the invisible sky under it. It is, to the end, a book of exploration, of searching regard. Its authenticity is deep in its language, not dependent on flash or effect: a grave, attentive holding of the light.

—W. S. Merwin

ACKNOWLEDGMENTS

I wish to thank the following individuals, without whose friendship and support the writing of this book would not have been possible: all my teachers, especially Lucie Brock-Broido; Chuck DeCroix, Keven Neff, Rick Olson, and George Corrie, for taking me into the cave on many after-hours trips; Johnny Merideth, Colleen O'Connor, Tres Seymour, and Charlie Hanion, for never getting tired of talking about Mammoth Cave; Joy Lyons, for being a wealth of information and unfailingly supportive; and Ted Lisowski, who weathered my moods from the beginning.

Grateful acknowledgment is made to the following publications, in which several poems in this collection have previously appeared:

The Missouri Review
"Ultima Thule"
"Freemartin"
"Dismantling the Cave Gate"
"Broken Country"
"Stephen Bishop's Grave"
"Cave Mummies"

No Roses Review
"Pond"
"The River and Under the River"
"Watermelons"

The Best American Poetry, 1996
"The River and Under the River"

Columbia Poetry Review
"Flowstone"
"Cave Wind"

The Harvard Advocate
"April Fifth, Nineteen Hundred Eighty-Three"

Insurance
"Kentucky"

In writing *Ultima Thule* I consulted a number of sources from which occasional phrases were taken and in some cases adapted. For information about the cave in the 1800s I relied on *Rambles in the Mammoth Cave,* by Alexander Clark Bullitt, and *One Hundred Miles in Mammoth Cave in 1880,* by H. C. Hovey. I also drew inspiration from works of a similar time period, most notably *Travels,* by William Bartram, the *Collected Works of Ralph Waldo Emerson,* and the writings of Henry David Thoreau.

I.
ULTIMA THULE

Stephen Bishop was the slave of Dr. John Croghan, owner of Kentucky's Mammoth Cave from 1839 to 1849. Bishop served as a guide at the cave from 1838 until 1857. Accounts of his daring explorations, which led to the discovery of miles of cave passageways, appeared in newspapers and books. His fame drew visitors from all over the world. By smoking their names onto the walls of the cave, he learned to read and write. Stephen Bishop died in 1857, at the age of thirty-seven. Oddly, the cause of his death was not recorded and remains unknown.

EXPLOR...

MAMMOTH

STEPHEN BISH...

Published by MORT...

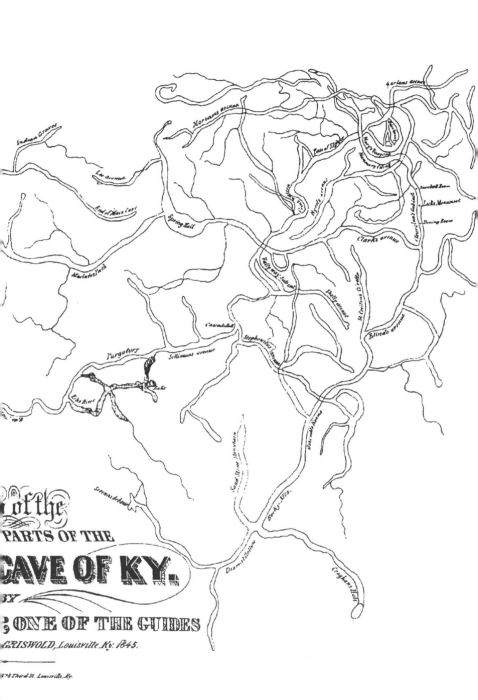

of the

PARTS OF THE

CAVE OF KY.

BY

ONE OF THE GUIDES

GRISWOLD, Louisville. Ky. 1845.

Candlewriting

Childhood was a mapless country, a rough
terrain of sinks and outcrops. Not once
did I suspect the earth was hollow, lost
as I was among the fields and shanties.
I remember the wind and how the sounds
it carried were my name, meant me, *Stephen* . . .
called out over the cornfield where I hid.
There was no sound when candlesmoke
met limestone—just this: seven characters
I learned to write with a taper on a stick.
What have they to do with that boy in the weeds?
Am I the letters or the hand that made them?
A word I answer to and turn from, or the flame
that holds the shadows, for a time at least, at bay?

Star Chamber

Once, the Doctor spoke to me at length
of stars and prognostications, how,
when we observe the waxing of the Moon,
everything cognate to her nature—marrow
in bones and in trees, flesh of the river
mussel—increases also. He told of tides
and how the ocean is affixed as with a chain
to moonlight. I think it must be different
in the Cave, where no light penetrates.
There, I have lost hours, whole cycles of the Sun.
At Star Chamber, I control the spheres—
a lantern hung just-so will produce the night sky
as if seen from a gorge; wobble it, and a comet,
smoky, pestilent, streaks across the Ether.

Visitations

There came to us, Tuesday last, a man
of most peculiar visage. The Doctor,
to whom we turned for insight, muttered
of abominations, dismissed our questions.
And yet I did not hesitate to show the Gentleman
as far in the Cave as his leisure and his pocket
would allow. For, there, to the faltering
glow of a greaselamp or candle, throng
shadows far more monstrous than he.
These I do not fear. It is the women
on the tours that give me pause, delicate,
ghost-white, how, that night, I'm told,
they wake to find themselves in unfamiliar
beds, and lost, bewildered, call my name.

Bottomless Pit

Before I crossed it on a cedar pole, legs
dangling into blackness, here the tours
would end: a loose and shingly precipice.
From my pack I would produce a scrap
of oiled paper, set fire to it, and send it
twisting and sputtering into the abyss.
I never saw it land, a flicker of light
on the fluted cistern. Soon I had found
the rivers beyond, their strange inhabitants
that emerged into the circle of my light
as if from another world, then vanished
at the least agitation of the water. *Touched,*
they said, *fish with no eyes!* until I sloshed
a pailful into light, reveled in their silence.

Echo River

Soon we had fashioned a rude boat,
and with lanterns affixed to the prow
were ferrying tours across the smoky waters:
Styx, Lethe, Echo River, the host
of wonders I had found. By slapping
the water with the flat of my paddle,
there comes a sound like the ringing of bells,
a mournful, hollow melody—waves lap-
ping and beating under the low stone arches.
The voice, too, will reproduce in myriad;
often I have led a tour in song, shouts raised
or pistols fired on the dark, deep water.
Children of a clanging, squeaking world,
we cannot bear the silence.

Shadow World

I am speaking of the shade of walls
and woods, the half-light on the dark side
of groves and fences—a region nearer
to the source of things, but always close at hand.
I have felt, of late, my shadow as an other
person there. Behold how the shades in the Cave
gather and deepen, extend in darker zones
from the center of the flame where I stand.
It was in such light that first my Charlotte came
to me. For a week I'd half expected her, until
at twilight, a shadow at the door, the sky waiting
a long time, pale and still, for the Moon
to rise. And afterwards, even the hemlocks
seemed foreign, their scent and turpentine.

Cartography

At Locust Grove, Great House, I pass days
in the garden—a stone bench, ornamental
cherries, August's dappled light. Once, a hawk's
shadow crossed my paper, startling me
from the dark rooms and corridors of my map,
an eye-draught of the known Cave passages.
The mind moves and the hand follows, as if
by torchlight on a moonless midnight, inking.
The Doctor is himself engaged in certain nightly
observations, plotting, by aide of lenses and tubes,
an atlas of the Moon, that distant, yellow orb,
yet closer, he says, than our own dark Continent:
its map made up of fringes and waterways, a dense,
vine-thick interior left blank. Uncharted.

Cave Formation

Safe from the withering glare of daylight,
a stone arbor, stone clusters of grapes.
I have heard more than one traveler
proclaim these encrustations coral-like.
Was once this place the bottom of a sea?
I think it must be so. How else explain
the salts that grow from joints in the rock:
Epsom, Glauber. Or what of the eyeless fish?
Stranded, perhaps, when the ocean vanished,
never again to join their kindred tribe
in that great salt realm. Who better to conjecture
on these matters than I? Theories I have learned
to keep from other, educated men,
lest they, like bats, fly shrieking at the torch-bearer.

Doctor Croghan

The Doctor draws the world to him by dint
of much imagination, fortunes spilled
to bring the *rudiments of culture* to this
poor backwater. At his bidding, oxcarts
bearing crates of wine will leave the coastline
of Virginia, clinking. The latest books
he brings that this place too might shine
as a center of learning and enterprise.
I have watched his projects grow, consume him—
hotelier, surgeon, gentleman farmer—
days when the light drains out of him,
and irritable, distant, he walks into
the orchard but finds, it seems, no peace
among the trees, his dream of ordered rows.

Brush Fire

A hot night, and the first breeze through my window
carried with it the whinny of a horse.
It had been so still, but suddenly the night
was restless, cocking its ear to a distant crackling,
a light, as of dawn, across the valley. To walk
abroad, and toward its source, was to swim
against a river of game, flushed from their roosts
in the oldest stands of timber, or from dens
in the tangled underbrush. By dawn,
forty acres had been consumed, the Hotel saved.
How strange when a party emerged from the Cave
at daybreak, blinking into the blue, smoke-
filled, ridgetop of embers—unaware
of the flames that all night raged above them.

Indian Mummy

If, as the Doctor believes, putrefaction
is the work of unquiet spirits hastening
to congregate with the air, she must have died
at peace, little Indian. Still dressed
in cloths of woven hemp, preserved,
she was displayed for a time in the Cave
where I found her. I will never forgive him
for selling her remains to a Mr. Nahum Ward,
purveyor of travelling curiosities,
oddments, a renowned Wonder Cabinet.
As I predicted, she never returned—lost,
they say, in a burning Museum,
a tiny spirit freed in ash and smoke . . .
safe at last from looters, learned men.

The Church

How soon the Cave forgets their worshipping,
a preacher and his flock, the great vault quiet.
Surely their God was here as he was not
in their sermon, words that have dissolved unheard.
I have stood at Pulpit Rock and felt the Cave
grow thick around me, as if for having
once been broken, it here became the essence
of itself. Nothing remains of their scattered
lights, of what they said or did. Nothing.
Where once the faithful came, a congregation
of bats, faint stirrings from the pews.
Gods too will be forgotten, exiled
to the pages of books. The Cave is praising them:
from the Organ Loft, vast chords of silence.

Dripstone

The Bengal Light is the most effective means
we have of driving darkness from the corners
where it lurks—a quick, blue flare that brought this day
a single drop of water to my gaze. Globe-like,
suspended, it held the scene about me in reverse:
a grotto glistening with nodules and globules.
Though not of the vegetable world, these
live and grow, and when struck, produce
melodious tones, liquid and wavering.
Mat and I had gone in search of specimens
for the Doctor's collection. How sad I grew
to see the changes wrought in them by sunlight.
How lustreless they appeared under glass,
their sparks extinguished, their music fled.

Tuberculosis Sanitarium

A taper burned at night, two stearine lights
by day—no way to gauge the weather here.
Such was their hope, distinct and inseparable
condition of the disease, that even when
reduced to shadows, they refused to quit
the Cave, insisted on their imminent return
to health. From the Doctor's monograph
on the curative virtues of the Cave came
stone huts, black drifts of smoke from cookfires,
their dry, hollow coughs. A colony of invalids.
I smuggled them plants against the Doctor's
commands that they should *take the cure
beyond the solar influences*—that grave
experiment. Unmentionable now.

Tours

The services of a guide cannot, as a rule,
be dispensed with; we alone can disentangle
the winding passageways. I will admit
the tours for me grow burdensome.
How long must I endure their need to fill
with talk the natural silence? I have heard
it all before, their proposed improvements:
Widen the trails so that two carriages
may pass abreast . . . here, a capacious ballroom.
Mere fancies. And yet beneath their words
I have discerned a kind of rough-hewn fear.
From drawing rooms and formal gardens
they come to me, from sunlit lives they enter
the chill, grand and instantaneous night.

River

The river is a wondrous machine. Haunt
of the Moon's changing face, it drifts among
the knobs and foothills: there, deep and fluid;
here, rippling over gravel beds. The water
swims with flesh—walleye, minnow. From nights
foggy and indeterminate rise mornings
when the Sun burns like a scald. On its banks
frogs pipe, the grass bends and rustles. It is
the singularity of chance and the shuffle
of things, stone basins where the chaff I've cast
on waters in the Cave emerged some several
hours hence. From the high stone bluffs nearby,
the water shines with an inner light—
makeshift, shifting, a candle in the current.

The Others

Thus far I have explored into the bowels
of the earth without impediment.
Others too would try—Materson, Nicholas,
those injudicious and eager for fame.
I've heard it said that yesterday, our Nick
was lowered by rope into the Maelstrom,
a pit of unknown depth. Those present claim
such shouts arose then from the chasm, the rope
was pulled until it fired by friction. A comedy.
I have seen the eyes he casts at her, and she
at him. This year I hardly note the seasons' turns:
first spring, and now the woodlands are awash
with summer. My thoughts remain unquiet,
here: low arch of the Netherworld, brooding.

Fame

It was the night before the night before last
when I sat so deep in thought by the fire.
The Doctor boasts I was the merest germ
of a man when he bought me. Through him,
I was able, in time, to acquire a knowledge
of science, a considerable degree of culture.
Through him, my fame—the subject of articles,
my map distributed widely. But fame,
like the fire in the hearth, must be fed:
a bundle of twigs soon needs a log to stay
alight. And then full thirty cords of oak.
I am ever in search of exploits, discoveries.
Some nights I wake in darkness to know
a greater darkness waits. A hillside. A mouth.

Ultima Thule

Above me even now the hills are bristling
with pine and cedar, dark branches shifting
in the rays of Sun or Moon; there, deep pools
receive their cave-cooled water, the Entrance
breathes its mingling airs, and, surely, somewhere,
Charlotte—stepping, perhaps, to the back porch
door at twilight. Absently. By habit.
I have felt the legend almost leave me.
Elbows, rucksack. No one has ever come
this far—a dusty, Hell-bent crawl, past pits
and keystones, to find myself deep in the ridge.
I was drawn to wonder, the margins of the map.
Breath and a heartbeat. A fading lamp.
I was coffled to the light.

II.
THE RIVER AND
UNDER THE RIVER

Ponds

The night we lost thirteen of them,
tremors shook along New Madrid fault.
In field after field the moon rose
to its own face echoed back,
cattle circling a crater's rim.
Along these margins, life had fixed —
an algal bloom, its underwater thud.
They were sucked through vast caverns.
In the Caveland, every pond's a fluke.
Let them be brief, then, as the land
gives up the ghost of fog, morning
in the sway-backed enclaves.
Already the clay dries and separates
along small faults. We expect no return.
Not even a tadpole's kink in mud
where Jesus bugs made miracles
the only way they could —
as if there were no underworld,
as if the pond would last.

Salts Cave

We slip the constant fifty-four
with ninety-eight point six, ten of us,
in the wobbling balance of lantern light.
We rattle and clink over breakdown
into rough-edged canyon, the cave
still holding a river's shape as it narrows
and deepens. And still the signs of life:
cane torches, half a gourd bowl,
and human feces — cold two thousand years.
They came here mining salts, the limestone walls
scripted with gypsum, epsomite, mirabilite.
We choose our steps, careful to leave no sign
of passing. Near Mummy Valley a flat slab
propped upright and markings —
turtle? dancing figure? map of the cave?
Twenty centuries and only one moment
when burnt torch end scraped limestone.
Mark, record, leave behind,
trace of what held heat, what is mine.

Cave Wind

Knowing it is shaped by
the size of the passage
it unwinds through (thus its
particular form and flue), we
are not deceived when, on
summer afternoons, it stiffens into
fog, clusters in the vines
and scrub brush littering the
entrance sink — no cough or
eructation, it is a constant
velocity we read or clock
(no need to vane it)
for the scope and girth
of the cavern, asking *does*
it go or siphon? knowing
its speed portends the cave
we'll discover, whether we will
walk or crawl, the breadth
of its breath, its given,
how, listening, we step into
the fricative, enter the socket
and proceed toward the lung
or bellows one half expects,
and, breathless, creep through the
throat of the longwinded earth.

Moonbow

My mother asks me to hold what of my childhood
fades like moonbow on that night we missed it,
clouds grey as fish above the Falls:
her pet peacock, how Lizzie tossed him
cornbread in the snow, called him Prettything
(a name that stuck), how he'd strut and fan
his tail. Remember? Later, a letter says she's sewing
prom dresses, the house flecked with sequins —
not since her father cleaned a mess of sun perch
in the kitchen, scattering their scales along the walls.
She spreads the pattern, smooths the taffeta folds,
constructing, dismantling, remembering fingers
raking out the entrails, a crisp and watery smell.

Sinking Stream

Though it leaks
across a space
not wide enough
to turn its jagged
bedload into
loaves and eggs,
its broken music
into song, the
course gets lost
among the twigs
and outcrops.
The wind that
rises out of bluff
and bottomland,
flaking and split-
ting, will hunt
the stream to this
lean animal: by
August it is glints
and rustlings — just
the spoor of water
to the bobcats
that will pass
along this barren
crust. It pours
through cracks

into the dark
and merges with
the roar of
buried currents.
Little room for
spreading skirts
of silt. Little
use to think of
source or end or
walk, as I have,
among rootwads
and thorns,
to find the cur-
rent dwindling
in a clot of leaves —
as if it could
be held by touch
or glittering
turn of phrase.

Floyd's Lost Passage

February 1925

Backlit and nervy, he bends at the cave mouth,
descends from the light past humps of moss
that tick inaudibly in the inverted skullcap
of the sink. Nothing moves in his wake.
Beancans knobbing the pockets of his coveralls,
small sustenance for the afterworld, he turns,
determined, from this one, feels his way
along splintery walls that rip at him, chafe
and paw him, the tight coil of his lank
loosens to their lusts and turns. Calloused hand
to limestone scallop, he crawls into the hollow
of a river's skeleton, and the muck wants him,
comes sweating to his touch. A switchback
and a siphon. The cave pinches down
to a sloping, narrow chute, and feet first,
the scuffed tip of his boot catches the rock that pins
his leg in the mud — a terminal breakdown
though the cave slinks on through the hills'
inhuman ribcage holding now
his looked for, soon-to-be-famous heart.

February 1995

I know they laid you out, waxen
and defaced, in the cave's first chamber,
and for a tip, they'd crack the lid —
high cheekbone, a rat-nibbled nose

in the lantern's slatted light.
One night the river took your stolen body
like a log, and still they hawked you
on the main road, ink-slung your inky end.
Complicit, I gape from greater distance
and worse light. Midnight spraddled
on your latest grave and I went looking
and felt nothing there — no disintegration,
no rest nor rekindling, just the great Flint Ridge,
white-knuckled in the half moon.

Floyd, you are the fox in its stump den,
you are the rattle in my wall.
I underestimate how close some nights
the cedars whittle on their Girkin shelves.
I want to think you're out there, if anywhere.
Nothing I can point to, nothing I can name.
What hole do you tend toward now,
what hard-won grave?

Kentucky

Blue heart, blue
vein, bluegrass
in wind. Near dawn,
a trickling. Paint
flake and darkened door.
Barn and blackshank.
A field of burley.
A lean-to.
Old lean man.
Green River
by john-boat, a trotline.
The fruit jar
near the fieldstone
wall. Channel cat,
gar. A cane
brake, a cave.
A road through
cedars. Fencerows.
Tents on a gravel bar —
campfire, grave.
Blood cross on door.
Damp curtain, hot
night, blue moon.
The house quiet:
the porchswing and the pie
safe. The hinge.

Plowpoint and spear.
Fossil, watercress,
worm. A cradle.
Blue corn, blue-
grass in wind, ocean
you once were.

April Fifth, Nineteen Hundred Eighty-Three

Brother came home in flood time, sudden
as the first heave of spring. That week
the river grew restless in its banks, tumbling
out chicken wire and empty bottles in its gorge.
Our house, too, strained, with one more in its tiny rooms:
Father, anxious and crop-hungry, paced the porch
as the waters rose, and Mother at the stove,
her face flushed, weathered our moods in silence.

When the rains broke we worked the bottomland,
Brother sneaking into town at night, proud new muscles
under his thin shirt. One afternoon, the tobacco finally
in the ground, I hid as he met a girl at the end of the road,
imagined words I could not speak — like finding a piano
in the barn, this possibility wide and tense as storm.

Watermelons

Pestered with sprays
and bedded in straw,
we are kept boys, swollen
like a bum knee; we look
like the bullfrog sounds.
Plugged with a knife
or zippered open wide,
tapped for our flaming insides.
We are water clocks,
weaned from the tube-footed vine,
hauled in by the load,
a tear-striped dirty child.
We cannot spill.
We wish we could read
the lightning on our hide,
the unhysterical thump
of a talking drum:
do not trust the speed of beauty
do not trust the beauty

Freemartin

In the fencelines it is already night, and so
not difficult to imagine that the shapes
moving there — the birds' last rustlings to their roost,
a coyote deep in grass — are moving under water.
Does the farm, at times like this, remember
the shoreline it once was, the hiss and spray
of that margin? Night after night,
a low moon climbs the cedars on the ridge;
its pale light floods the bottomland, drifts
and pools and finds a herd of cattle wading
through alfalfa. In brakes of cane,
the river dismantles an ancient masonry,
vast tides of limestone, the water cross-cutting
the buried currents. A waxing smudge
of light floats across the ripples and eddies,
and yet it will not jar the bedrock's memory,
or raise strange creatures from the stone.
Night itself is like stone, an aggregate
of twitch and spark that hardens in the fencelines.
Through it, too, a river flows: river of blood,
river of milk, the cattle spooked and circling.
The moon calls out to what is water and what is water
answers. A pale face in the cedars. A bleat.
Something somewhere calcifies.

Flowstone

How the water behaves
determines their shape and composition:
stalactites, a rimstone dam.
Above, great fossil slabs
slough off in geologic time,
limestone leached and percolating
into caverns. At a cubic inch
per century, this is cave-making
in reverse. But to what end?
A caver pushing virgin passage
out beyond the sandstone lip
emerges into verticals, hung
and glinting where his carbide falls.
Is it for this or the process?
What an ancient sea set down in even lines
is worked into a cursive scrawl,
as run-off through the bedding planes
recalls
a steamy day, an inland sea,
the continent adrift —
south of the equator but bearing north.

The River and Under the River

At dusk every day, our cattle leave the river,

single-file, trundling their weight to the upper pastures.

And every night, the river is left to itself, infertile

and self-loathing, most beautiful when it comes close

to absence; its grooves and grottoes hum

with the noise of a landscape's slow consumption.

If I put my ear to the ground

could I hear the drag of the river turning

limestone into silt? Would it tell of Carlos pulled

through water on a slim and muscly night at Turnhole Bend?

I want to know the missing part of his story

that ends with the flush of foxfire on a grave —

as if from the body's heat fading out.

Tonight the river is at work dissolving, solving

over and over the riddle of its loosening.

I want to know how to hear it, and what it might teach me:

how to inhabit this thing of bone, gut, and blood,

this part of me that would not vanish if I vanished.

III.

THE DARK COUNTY

Dismantling the Cave Gate

It started with the clang of plates and girders,
one last click of the rusted turnstile,
and then a river of breath had come loose
into the night. The workmen claim it took
the hats from their heads, blew out their lights,
and for a moment they had stood in darkness,
listening to the cave's unearthly moan.
It was a sound not heard in over fifty years
that rippled out into the undergrowth,
whistled across the limestone lintel, and rose—
a rustling, vast and unfamiliar to the bats
beneath the streetlamps and underpasses,
who gathered it in their ears and followed,
dark and fluttering, to the fluttering dark.

June

In the weird back country I come home to,
in its broad alluvial flats and cockleburs,
in the wind that trestles the leaves, yes,
somewhere, lost among the moonlight
falling thick and copper on the river's fan
of chert, I was the lantern slipping at dusk
along a hidden path, a shift in the wind-
vane at the Entrance, or the spike I made
in its readout just by standing at the gate
near midnight—unaccounted for, anomalous.
I was a length of days, a gathering of dust.
I was so far then from those months of self-
congratulation. Home again, changed again,
and nothing, not one thing, had been resolved.

Farming

Our hayloft was the last refuge of order:
in its brown gloom we brought the upstart provinces
of summer to their knees, bound them in twine,
and hauled them to the cattle at the troughs.
We kept its square bales stacked and reachable.
My father stands in the barn's wide upper doors,
flicks a cigarette into the twilight, and scans
the fields for what we both know lies in wait:
chaos with its many names—frost or drought
or thistles or the herd that breaks the fence.
At my feet the cave lay open and unchanged,
the dry trunk passage where I touched a cane
that grew when Rome had sacked Jerusalem,
its burnt end blackening my thumb.

Broken Country

Some nights I drive the backroads out across
the county, its knobs and barrens spreading
huge and oddly weightless in the hot black air.
I'd forgotten how, each August, the fields rise up
at every turn like walls in the headlights,
how so much of the world lies out of reach.
Now only the wind can comb its knitted stalks,
only the bats that beat across a fence of light
can thread its ductwork—as we did, that once,
standing shoulder to shoulder in the glint
of New Discovery; we were intruders there
inside that lost cave passage, turning at last
to face the long walk back, to let our thick lives
come between us and that thin, lightless place.

Solution Cave

When sunlight shook across the ripples
or a snag, the river turned as green
as bottle glass. It was limestone, of course,
prismatic and dissolved, that churned
past trotlines, watercress, in and out
of shadow. The river spools out glimpses
of a vast hydraulics, the water's complex
(though unmagical) journey from caprock
to stalactite, from rain into the pitch-black
torrents of the aquifer. I paddled the canoe
past soft mud banks and roots, leaned back,
and tried for once to take it all on faith:
the distant rookeries of stone, the farms
where sinkholes open like stigmata in the grass.

Premonitions

The summer harbored darkness in its width
and light; as fields hold barns, so August
kept the umbers of a fading rain. Nothing
was what it seemed. A helmet, a headlamp,
too many days spent crossing and recrossing
that perimeter where the sun short-circuits,
where the veins of sap and pigment end.
In the cave I could forget how the season
above me flirted with autumn. I'd thought
it was a matter of vigilance to watch
the sunlight splattering the road
and find a fate of car wrecks, or to discover
in the rub and link of a sycamore's limbs
an inkling, unacknowledged, of her with him.

Comet Hale-Bopp

To find it in the cut of sky above the Entrance
was to know, as I had not, of thin blue nights
and howling dark, and what sifts out
across four thousand winters. That night
again, the thunder of a herd had dwindled
across the tills and drifts of centuries, again
the smoke from cookfires rose along its wake,
and hid dark faces drifting toward a rockshelter.
They put their splintered tools into the dirt,
set crops by the clock of the sky, and so it was
that a smudge of light had crossed the stars
at the ridgeline, that someone picked their way
down broken slabs, lit a torch, and marked
the instant that a vast and inner darkness shattered.

Pushing a Lead

We'd found the blowhole down a jagged shaft
and followed it—on our hands and knees,
through mud and dust and splintered chert,
the passage tightening to a flat-out belly-crawl.
The wind we followed down the south flank
of the ridge should have meant big cave,
though we never found it in the maze
of canyonwalks and chimneys. I watched the walls
for fossils as we went: defunct coral stems,
and thought of all the limestone up above us,
an ocean of it, grey and green and rocking
in the moonlight. We wedged and swam
against its currents like a school of headlamps,
lost and tiny, at the ink-black bottom of a sea.

Stephen Bishop's Grave

It took four summers here for me to realize
the cave looped back under the Old Guide
Cemetery, that what was mortal floated
in a crust of brittle sandstone or leaked
into the darkest rivers and was caving still.
I went that drizzling night to stand
where the paper-trail he left had vanished:
woodsmoke, mist, a mossed-over name.
I knew enough by then to know that he,
of all people, would prefer the company of rain
to my own, but I went anyway, thinking
of my pale inventions, and stood a long time,
vigilant for his shadow in my own,
his voice as it differed from the wind.

51

Cave Mummies

Their faces will remain lost in the shadows
of the dry cane-reeds they lit and held aloft.
What comes down to us is mortal, dust—
their intact hair and fingernails, their teeth
worn to the gums by mussels full of sand.
We've probed their last meals matted in their guts
and joined a history of side-show men
who blurred into the archaeologists I've met.
They bend like surgeons in the lantern's light,
but do they ever stop, I've wondered, stare out
into the dark, and ask what brought us here,
all of us, what artifact will tell the future
of a longing wild and inarticulate,
of a dark place loved and gotten in the blood?